God Is Always with You

written by Allia Zobel Nolan

illustrated by Trace Moroney

KREGEL
Kidzone
Where Kids are number One

Kregel Publications • Grand Rapids, Michigan

"Mama, where does God live?" Little Panda asked.

"Well, Little Panda," Mama said, "God lives in heaven and in the hearts of those who believe in his Son, Jesus."

"Does that mean God is with me here in my lookout tree?"

"Yes, Little Panda. God is always with you."

Little Panda climbed down from the tree. What Mama said had
started him thinking.

"But doesn't God have a zillion more important things to do?"
he said.

"*You* are one of the most important things to God,"
said Mama. "He loves you as much as I do—even more."
"Really, Mama?" said Little Panda. "Wow!"

Little Panda climbed up his slide while his imagination took him high up Mount Everest.

"But what if I went mountain climbing far away?" he asked.
"Would God be with me there?"

"Yes, dear," Mama said. "God would be with you in the mountains.
But," she said, "he'd probably want you to wear something warm."

"Like my jacket?" Little Panda said.

"Right," said Mama. "God is always with you and he loves you like I do."

Little Panda went to the pond with his boat. He watched it glide
in the water, while he daydreamed of greater adventures.

"But what if I sailed way out on the high seas?" Little Panda asked.
"Would God be with me there?"

"Of course," Mama said, strolling to the pond. "You could sail this whole world, and God would be with you. But, he'd probably want you to be careful."

"So I don't fall in the water, Mama?"

"Right," said Mama. "God is always with you and he loves you like I do."

Little Panda stood out in the rain, playing with his rubber toy.

But in his mind, he was battling a purple dragon.

"But what if I left and went to fight a big monster?" Little Panda called over his shoulder. "Would God be with me there?"

"Yes, dear," Mama answered. "You could battle an army of dragons and
God would be with you. But, he'd probably want you to wear your boots."

"So I wouldn't catch cold, Mama?"

"Right," said Mama. "God is always with you and he loves you like I do."

Little Panda took a ride on the tree swing while he pretended
to soar around the world.

"But what if I flew high in the sky?" Little Panda asked.
"Would God still be with me?"

"You bet," said Mama. "You could fly around the whole world and God would be with you. But he'd probably want you to eat before you go."

"My dinner. Right, Mama?"

"Right," said Mama. "God is always with you and he loves you like I do."

Little Panda hopped off the swing. He took off his jacket, picked some bamboo, and disappeared. Mama called him in to eat. He didn't come, so she went to find him.

Little Panda saw her and took her hand. "Can God see me
right now, too, Mama?" he asked, pulling her behind the tree.
"Yes, dear," Mama answered.

"Good," said Little Panda, pointing to a bamboo heart on the ground, "because I made him something, you know, for always being with me. Think he'll like it, Mama?"

"Yes, Little Panda." Mama said. Then she gave him a big hug.